VOCAL SELECTIONS
FROM

Music by
CY COLEMAN

Lyrics by
MICHAEL STEWART

C • O • N • T • E • N • T • S

THERE IS A SUCKER BORN EV'RY MINUTE

Music by
CY COLEMAN

Lyrics by
MICHAEL STEWART

1. There is a suck - er _____ born ev - 'ry min - ute, _____
2. Each bless - ed hour _____ brings six - ty of 'em _____
3. There is a suck - er _____ born ev - 'ry min - ute, _____

THANK GOD I'M OLD

Music by
CY COLEMAN

Lyrics by
MICHAEL STEWART

9

12

THE COLORS OF MY LIFE

Music by
CY COLEMAN

Lyrics by
MICHAEL STEWART

ONE BRICK AT A TIME

Music by
CY COLEMAN

Lyrics by
MICHAEL STEWART

17

20

MUSEUM SONG

Music by
CY COLEMAN

Lyrics by
MICHAEL STEWART

Very bright

Quite a lot-ta
Ar - ma - dil - las,

Ro-man ter - ra cot-ta,
clev-er cat - er - pil - lars,

Liv-in' la - va from the
Re - pro - duc - tions of the

flanks of Et - na.
Cy - clops' ret - 'na.

Stat - u - ar - y
Crys-tal blow-in',

ride a drom-e - dar - y,
au - to - mat - ic sew-in',

I LIKE YOUR STYLE

Music by
CY COLEMAN

Lyrics by
MICHAEL STEWART

No shouts or quar - rels,

No blows _____ or tears. _____

One sim - ple fuss to dis - sect and dis - cuss, for the

LOVE MAKES SUCH FOOLS OF US ALL

Music by
CY COLEMAN

Lyrics by
MICHAEL STEWART

BIGGER ISN'T BETTER

Music by
CY COLEMAN

Lyrics by
MICHAEL STEWART

OUT THERE

Music by
CY COLEMAN

Lyrics by
MICHAEL STEWART

Staying home, living day by day may be safe but it
Turning back should the high-way bend, turning down every

can't be duller, Seeing things only black and gray
chance you're given, Takes the risk out of life, but friend,

COME FOLLOW THE BAND

Music by
CY COLEMAN

Lyrics by
MICHAEL STEWART

Vigorously

f

mf

G11   C   Cmaj7   C6   G7

Come Fol -low The Band ___ where ev - er it's at, ___

C   E7   F   Eb7

Let both of your feet ___ beat time to the drum ___ and feel your

BLACK AND WHITE

Music by
CY COLEMAN

Lyrics by
MICHAEL STEWART

53

THE PRINCE OF HUMBUG

Music by
CY COLEMAN

Lyrics by
MICHAEL STEWART

JOIN THE CIRCUS

Music by
CY COLEMAN

Lyrics by
MICHAEL STEWART

64

Read - y to roam ____ a - gain, read - y to stray. ____
Shoul - der your pack ____ and then hitch up the shay. ____
Read - y to roam ____ a - gain, read - y to stray. ____

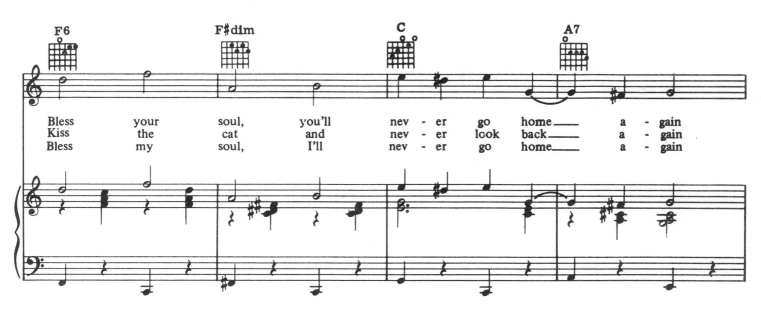

Bless your soul, you'll nev - er go home ____ a - gain
Kiss the cat and nev - er look back ____ a - gain
Bless my soul, I'll nev - er go home ____ a - gain

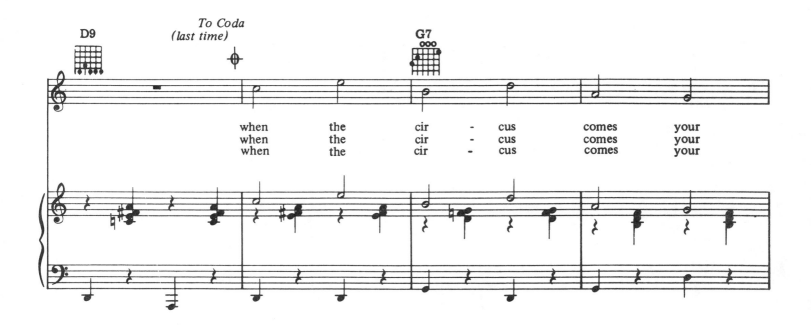

when the cir - cus comes your
when the cir - cus comes your
when the cir - cus comes your